ZEN ART FOR MEDITATION

ZEN ART

FOR MEDITATION

by STEWART W. HOLMES
and CHIMYO HORIOKA

CHARLES E. TUTTLE COMPANY
Rutland, Vermont   Tokyo, Japan

Published by the Charles E. Tuttle Company, Inc.
of Rutland, Vermont & Tokyo, Japan
with editorial offices at
Suido 1-chome, 2-6, Bunkyo-ku, Tokyo

Copyright in Japan, 1973
by Charles E. Tuttle Co., Inc.

Library of Congress Catalog Card No. 73-78279
International Standard Book No. 0-8048-1255-1

First printing, 1973
Twelfth printing, 1990

PRINTED IN JAPAN

TABLE OF CONTENTS

TABLE OF CONTENTS

LIST OF ILLUSTRATIONS

LIST OF ILLUSTRATIONS

ACKNOWLEDGMENTS

Acknowledgment is made to the following for permission to use reproductions of the paintings included here:

Kozan-ji, Kyoto: plate 26
Nanzen-ji, Kyoto: plate 30
Ryusen-an, Hanazono Myoshin-ji, Kyoto: plate 25
Mr. Nagachika Asano, Tokyo: plate 23
Mr. Sotaro Kubo, Izumi: plate 16
Mr. Takaharu Mitsui, Tokyo: plate 24
Mr. Tomijiro Nakamura, Tokyo: plate 14
Mr. Fumihide Nomura, Kyoto: plate 12
Hakone Museum: plates 20, 21
Maeda Ikutoku-kai, Tokyo: plate 4
Museum of Fine Arts, Boston: plates 1, 2, 3, 7, 8, 9, 10, 11, 15, 17, 18, 19, 22, 27, 28, 31
Tokyo National Museum: plates 6, 29
Yamato Bunka Museum, Nara: plates 5, 13

For permission to use quoted passages acknowledgment is also made to the following:

Alfred A. Knopf, Inc., for a passage from "A Farewell to Meng Hao-an on His Way to Yang-Chou," by Li Po, translated by Witter Bynner, quoted from *The Jade Mountain: A Chinese Anthology* (New York: 1929).

Rider & Co. and the executors of the late D. T. Suzuki, for the passages quoted from *Essays in Zen Buddhism*, first series (London: 1970), and *Essays in Zen Buddhism*, second series (London: 1970), by D. T. Suzuki.

We wish to thank Mrs. Yasuko Horioka for creating fresh translations of the haiku. Her scholarship and empathy were invaluable in finding the right haiku and in establishing an authoritative version of each.

ACKNOWLEDGMENTS

INTRODUCTION

This book is meant for those who wish to own reproductions of some of the finest pictorial art in the Zen tradition, in a format favorable to participation in the artists' vision.

Hundreds of pictures from the canon of classical Chinese and Japanese ink painting were examined to find thirty-one that would appeal to Western viewers and would also present a wide spectrum of subjects and styles. The originals of this gallery-without-walls exhibition are in collections all over the world. These private and national treasures are widely considered to be not only great works of art but also portraits of various faces of man's soul.

From this it follows that this book is also for those who wish, by meditating somewhat in the Zen way, to experience certain insights into human nature and the universe. To this end it provides for each picture a commentary focused on a Zen tenet and illuminated by haiku poems. Thus great masterpieces by Zen-inspired artists and poets, used and preserved for centuries by followers of the Zen Way, are here made available to Westerners as stimuli to expansions of consciousness. The book may function as a substitute (admittedly quite inadequate) for the guidance of a Zen master.

● *Using the Book*

Whether you are primarily interested in enjoying great examples of the Chinese and Japanese art of ink painting (*sumi-e*) or in achieving expansions of consciousness and preconsciousness, this book opens doors.

If you wish to use it as a meditation instrument, the following sequence is suggested as a model on which to build your own practice.* You will doubtless make your own adaptations as time goes on.

1. PLACE: a softly lighted room, moderate in temperature, quiet, and otherwise suitable for a serene state of mind.
2. CLOTHING: loose, comfortable—or none.
3. MODE OF SITTING: the nearest possible approximation to the lotus position (see pictures of statues of the seated Buddha). Even if you find a chair more comfortable at first, try to get accustomed to sitting cross-legged on the floor.

   Sit on a thick, firm pillow so that your buttocks are higher than your knees. If you can finally manage to sit with your left foot on your right thigh, you will find that putting a thinner pillow under your left knee will help to keep both knees on something firm.

   Think of your main weight as being in your lower body, while your upper body (above the navel) seems weightless. Be very erect, but not ramrod rigid. Have the tension of the alert athlete, not of the soldier at attention.

For a minute or so after you seat yourself, while the whirl inside you gradually slows down, let an awareness of the pleasure of being quiet—externally and internally—pervade you. Taking some slow, deep breaths will help.

When you feel ready, take up the picture you have chosen for this occasion and read the accompanying meditation and haiku poems once or twice. Look closely at the picture so that both its general aspects and its details are imprinted on your mind. After you are tuned

* These items are largely taken from notes made by Zen Master Yasutani for his students. A rather complete statement may be found in Philip Kapleau's *The Three Pillars of Zen* (New York: 1966).

in to it, place it, propped up if necessary, where you can see it easily.

Now you are going to enter into a more intimate transaction with it. As your mind plays with the ideas and images in the meditation, let your eyes roam around the picture. At this stage you may find that you're talking to yourself about the picture or about something you recall from the commentary. Try to keep your talk from being of an evaluating, judging kind. Open yourself.

As you open yourself to the "message" of the commentary and to the picture, let your own verbalizings gradually die away. To reduce the chatter, you will find it helpful to let your eyes wander very slowly and patiently over each detail of the painting, even to noting how individual brush strokes were made. When the chatter starts up again, you may find it valuable to devote part of your mind to counting while you go through the breathing cycle of inhale, hold, exhale. Listening to the tick-tock of a pendulum clock or metronome will give a hypnotic regularity to your count.

If the transaction is developing well, you may begin to feel the alertness of the heron watching for a frog, the soaring quality of mountain peaks rising up out of valley mists into the sky, the quiet serenity of a sage sitting in a shelter looking out over a mountain lake. The Zen tenet, as developed in the commentary, may be exercising its influence either below or just above the threshold of your consciousness. You can be sure that the Zen orientation as expressed in picture, haiku, and commentary is to some degree restructuring your mind patterns.

After a minute or two—or more—you may find thoughts not associated with the picture or tenet arising in your mind. This occurs quite naturally. As Master Yasutani says, "[Zen meditation] does not aim at making the mind inactive, but at quieting and unifying it in the midst of activity."

Put a pencil and paper beside you, to record thoughts that you will want to recall later; then you will free yourself from the effort of trying to remember them. Casual thoughts and reactions to the environment will pass through your mind and leave no effect. Judgments, beliefs, ideologies are not so innocuous; if possible, avoid them.

It will help to keep your eyes open and fastened "idly" about three feet in front of you on the floor. It may also help to count as you inhale and exhale.

Strike a happy medium between floating with what happens in a relaxed way and keeping an alert awareness of yourself as an organism solidly poised in athletic tension.

● *What Is Zen?*

Before we speak more specifically about the commentaries, or meditations, we should consider briefly what *Zen* means as it is used here. The word *Zen* is the Japanese form of the Chinese word *Ch'an*, which is the Chinese form of the Indian *Dhyana*, meaning a particular kind of meditation. The Buddha, 2,500 years ago in India, taught the importance of this kind of meditation in achieving enlightenment. A thousand years later, we are told, Bodhidharma, an Indian missionary, took this message to China. There, followers of Lao Tzu assimilated it to their way of life, called Taoism. Their attitude of going along with the nature of things, the Tao, harmonized with the non-self-assertive, noncraving acceptance of life as taught originally in India by the Buddha and then in China by Bodhidharma. The Dhyana meditation being at the heart of Bodhidharma's Buddhism, this school of Buddhism was called Ch'an. Ch'an Buddhism was tremendously influential in Chinese culture. The great arts of the Sung dynasty in China (960–1280) were created primarily by Ch'an-trained people.

When monks brought Ch'an to Japan in the twelfth century, it developed even more rapidly and influenced the culture even more profoundly than it had in China. Called Zen by its Japanese converts, it shaped not only the religion of the people but also the orientation of the creative workers in sculpture, painting, architecture, landscape gardening, house furnishing, the theater—even bushido, the code of the warrior, and the "arts" of swordsmanship and archery. Its selfless respect for the nature of things—like wood, rocks, clay, moss, streams, pools—as being, equally with human beings, aspects of Buddha-nature, produced a great tradition characterized by distinguished lives and distinguished works of art.

This seedbed of unselfconscious felicity and creativity is still available to us through the works of art and the tradition of meditation created by the Zen masters.

Since Zen looks beyond the symbol to the thing, the stereotypes that most of us have constructed concerning color, sex, and age, as well as the dogmas of ethnic-bound cultures, are seen to be manmade, not part of the nature of things. Each person is structured, or "coded," to live best in his particular transaction with the Great Tao; he has his private Tao. As each of us opens himself to the operation of his secret code, he progressively functions more harmoniously. Sitting erect, quietly and strongly, in a suitable environment, facilitates this opening. The same inner coding or wisdom that heals a cut or mends a broken bone can heal the psychic wounds that each of us suffers.

● *The Zen Orientation*

Up through the centuries since the Buddha's time, a very large number of people in the Far East have searched for the way or ways in which this code operates. With their own beings as laboratories, they have conducted numberless experiments. Out of this work, especially since Bodhidharma's union of Taoism and Buddhism, has come a body of ideas and attitudes and a set of techniques to facilitate the operation of the code. This approach is what we call Zen.

The Zen way of living may be applied in any field of human endeavor—business, art, teaching, farming, carpentering, parenting, housekeeping. Actually, it would be more accurate to say that men and women can live according to the Zen way in various fields of human endeavor. For this is not a trick to be applied to increase one's output or one's degree of happiness. Rather, it becomes a total reorientation to one's whole array of behaviors.

In the approach to Zen developed in this book, you will have for consideration a series of fifteen tenets representing aspects of this orientation. To help you experience these tenets you will have two pictures for each of them, each with its commentary and haiku. While you are looking at these "landscapes of the soul," meanings of the tenet for each picture will be becoming clearer and richer inside you. The way you are sitting, the way you are looking, the way you are reacting to the stimuli will all facilitate the structuring of this aspect of Zen. The work of building new insights will go on primarily below the threshold of consciousness.

● *Zen Tenets*

TENET 1: The realities of the life are most truly seen in everyday things and actions.

TENET 2: Everything exists according to its own nature. Our individual perceptions of worth, correctness, beauty, size, and value exist inside our heads, not outside them.

TENET 3: Everything exists in relation to other things.

TENET 4: The self and the rest of the universe are not separate entities but one functioning whole.

TENET 5: Man arises from nature and gets along most effectively by collaborating with nature, rather than trying to master it.

TENET 6: There is no ego in the sense of an endlessly enduring, unchanging private soul or personality that temporarily inhabits the body.

TENET 7: True insight does not issue from specialized knowledge, from membership in coteries, from doctrines or dogmas. It comes from the preconscious intuitions of one's whole being, from one's own code.

TENET 8: In emptiness, forms are born. When one becomes empty of the assumptions, inferences, and judgments he has acquired over the years, he comes close to his original nature and is capable of conceiving original ideas and reacting freshly.

TENET 9: Being a spectator while one is also a participant spoils one's performance.

TENET 10: Security and changelessness are fabricated by the ego-dominated mind and do not exist in nature. To accept insecurity and commit oneself to the unknown creates a relaxing faith in the universe.

TENET 11: One can live only in the present moment.

TENET 12: Living process and words about it are not the same and should not be treated as equal in worth.

TENET 13: When we perceive the incongruity between theories about life and what we feel intuitively to be true on the nonverbal, nonjudging plane, there is nothing to do but laugh.

TENET 14: Zen art has this characteristic quality, that it can fuse delight in a work of visual art, knowledge of life, and personal experiences and intuitions into one creative event.

TENET 15: Each of us develops into a unique individual who enters into unique transactions with the world as it exists for him.

● *Experiencing a Haiku and a Picture*

How may we experience a haiku? Let us read this one by Joso:

> Fields and mountains
> All taken by the snow;
> Nothing remains.*

The composer of a haiku characteristically gives us nothing but a picture, a vignette of a tiny part of the panorama of life as he sees it. If there are nonpictorial implications, it is up to us to create them.

Let us imagine a mental image based on the words of this haiku. A whiteness covers all—all the brooks and bushes and ledges and trees and houses. Individual forms have been smoothed over or obliterated. After visualizing this, open yourself to a feeling of the emp-

* Except where other translators are identified, all translations in this volume are by Yasuko Horioka.

tiness of this landscape. You are faced with—nothing. Instead of picturing a brook here and a stone wall there and a straw-thatched house under a mountain crag, you see only white undulations. With nothing in particular to stimulate your pictorial imagination, you just sit there.

In this quiet sitting, you are opening yourself to what Zen-trained people mean when they say that emptiness is fullness or that emptiness is the womb of forms. Under that mantle of snow exist innumerable forms—leaf buds waiting to open, hibernating animals, bacteria, lichen and mosses on rocks, seeds of grasses, streams in their rocky beds. Each exists there ready to grow and move according to the laws of its own life; each is a different expression of the primal energy. Analogously, when our conscious verbalizing, our almost incessant chatter is stilled, the wiser part of us, as an atom of the primal energy, has a chance to develop.

Joso did not say all this. But the stone he dropped into the pool of our awareness created these ripples: these, and doubtless many others in other minds.

Now let us look at a picture (plate 1, p. 19) and see what we see. Eight hundred years ago, in Sung-dynasty China, a Zen man painted it. Do you see a great swirl of motion? Do your eyes follow the curves of the flock of birds coming in to roost in the big tree for the night? Do you follow the slanting crest of the mountain and the dark ridge of the hill and pick up the little cataract and follow the stream as it flows past the base of the tree? And then do you follow the bare branches that spread out from the trunk in lines that bend over and form a circle of protection for that little thatch-roofed cottage? Who lives in this center of tranquillity in the midst of the energetic landscape? We see no one. How mysterious this is: movement—no movement; life—no life; things—no thing.

After you have let this symbol permeate you for a bit, consider this idea: "There is process; there is stillness. But there is no endlessly enduring, unchanging private soul in the midst of the process." Don't argue with this idea. Just let it germinate.

And then enjoy the peace that follows.

Plate 1.

● *Conclusion*

This sample of the mind-expanding function of the meditation aspect of this book will give an idea of the possibilities to be found herein. While it would be presumptuous and quite false to say that using the book in this way will result in enlightenment, such use may be for many people the best feasible way to get some experience of Zen. Few Westerners have access to a Zen master. The numerous books on Zen are more likely to provide an intellectual understanding of the aims and methods of Zen than the feel of Zen insights. But it is these insights that are most likely to help us find that order and meaning in our life to which the words and actions of many Zen-trained people bear witness.

Apart from this meditation aspect, the likelihood of your participating in the artists' vision is greatly enhanced by this empathic, non-analytic approach. You and each artist come together in a creative transaction that transcends the limitations of time and culture.

ZEN TENETS

EVERYDAY THINGS

Tenet 1: *The realities of life are most truly seen in everyday things and actions.*

PLATE 2: Here is a picture painted in China about eight hundred years ago, showing a somewhat elderly and somewhat inebriated gentleman returning from a feast. The gay decorations on his hat are frazzled, his party robe is rumpled, his face is grizzled and mizzled. He remains upright on the water buffalo's back only with the assistance of a young attendant. Such an event some might find reprehensible, disgusting, ridiculous. But let's open ourselves to the whole picture.

The huge weeping willow tree bends gracefully above the old man. The buffalo, secured through the nose with a taut line held by a stoop-shouldered attendant, proceeds as slowly as possible, mournful of mien, shaggy of coat, and scrawny of tail. The attendant is completely impassive. The roadside plants go right on growing. Everything is fulfilling its part in the whole. Such is life—and of such are the realities of life. Harmony comes in understanding things on their own terms, and in a compassionate and humorous acceptance of the way they fulfill their roles.

The artist's technique contributes to this feeling of the universal in the particular. The strokes he uses to make the plant and willow leaves, the rocks and bits of vegetation, the buffalo's hairs and hooves, are quite conventional. Even the clothes and faces seem casually drawn with a few strokes of a fine brush. Yet one feels close to this particular tree, to this old man with his self-inflicted headache and addled wits, to this buffalo, pressed into duty as a taxi after serving long hours as a tractor. Here is no academic exercise, but a slice of life as it has been lived by Everyman for thousands of years. This is the way things are on planet Earth, our only home.

*

Plate 2.

Shiki must have been intensely aware, intensely alive, when he had the experience described in this haiku:

> Oh, how I enjoy
> Eating a persimmon
> While Horyu temple bells boom.

You can almost feel with him the vibrations entering his ears and the juices running down his gullet. He was really living.

> The rainy season!
> The doorway is flooded
> And the frogs are swimming there.
> —SAMPU

What a way to react to one's house being flooded! Yet can you think of a better way? The rains come; the flood waters rise; into your entryway come not only buckets of water but frogs. So you sit and watch the frogs swim.

> Moon adrift in a cloud:
> Why don't I borrow
> A little juicy melon?
> —SHIKI

A cloud happens to darken the moonlit landscape. There happens to be a melon patch right here. And it would be borrowing, not stealing. So—who's counting? Man cannot live by moon viewing alone.

This is indeed the way things are on planet Earth.

PLATE 3: How remote from the everyday world this landscape seems! Out of the river valley that disappears mysteriously into

Plate 3.

Detail, Plate 3.

infinity rise skyshouldering mountains. Their serrated summits soar disembodied out of the valley mists. Earthly processes of gravitation, geological formation, and plant life seem unrelated to these precipices. The unreal becomes actual here; the world of everyday experience is unreal or, at most, insignificant.

Then the exploring eye comes upon a little figure at the lower right, a traveler with his bundle on a stick over his shoulder. He's heading for an inn standing on piles over a little bay. A closer examination reveals people sitting in the inn. Further back under a wooded hill, we can see more houses, hugging the ground. The bay, the houses, and a somewhat rickety plank bridge are all framed by the bare branches of an old willow.

All at once we feel more at ease, as we realize that the scene does include everyday things and actions. Strange as the landscape may have seemed at first, it does after all belong to our familiar earth. Human beings built that bridge and that inn to which it leads. And a weary traveler seeks refuge there, as many have before him.

Here are the realities that endure for us human beings across the centuries. A bridge spans the mysteriously infinite river; under the surrealistic crags, an inn awaits the traveler. There, at the end of the day, at the misty close of half a global rotation, wait a tasty bowl of soup, perhaps, and a good broiled fish.

*

Even the general
Took off his armor to gaze
At our peonies.
                    —KIKAKU

Of course, Kikaku's peonies may not have been everyday peonies.

Well, the fall typhoon
Has taken its first victim.
The local scarecrow.
                    —KYOROKU

The fall of Kyoroku's humble scarecrow gives significance to an event of planetary scope—the typhoon.

If I could bundle
Fuji's breezes back to town.
What a souvenir!
                    —BASHO

Basho makes fun of one of man's most fundamental and enduring instincts—collecting. And, while collecting souvenirs may be commonplace, what more powerful device can we muster against that devastating reality, all-devouring time?

PERCEPTIONS

Tenet 2: *Everything exists according to its own nature. Our individual perceptions of worth, correctness, beauty, size, and value exist inside our heads, not outside them.*

PLATE 4: What a ridiculous foursome! A grossly fat man drowsing contentedly while leaning on a tiger. Tiger sleeping happily. Fat boys leaning on man and hence on tiger. Tigers should be prowling pridefully, looking for prey. Men should be at work, setting good examples to youthful apprentices.

Should they? Well, yes—if they live according to our stereotypes. But such stereotypes are inside, not outside, our heads. This tiger's nature is different. This tiger likes to snooze with his paws crossed peacefully, feeling the warm weight of soft human bodies. He likes this, apparently, so it must be in accord with his nature.

And it is the nature of his friends to enjoy his company in perfect trust. They have found a spot pleasing to them all, beside a quiet stream, protected by a steep bank. Here they recline, getting fatter and lazier and happier by the minute. By "civilized" standards they have little worth, little beauty of body or mind. Yet they have come to terms with themselves. We might say the tiger of the desire to dominate is asleep in them, letting them relax. They are all at one with their basic natures, as you can see by the harmony written on their relaxed, faintly smiling faces.

Each one of us—sage, tiger, man on the street—exists on other levels than the conscious one. We say, "It came to me that . . . " or "A thought just popped into my mind." Where did these thoughts come from? Can we answer this question by saying, "From the same place that the directions for body growth and repair come from"? That is to say, they come from our inner nature, that makes

豊干抱虎睡拾得
寒山打作一塲懡㦬大
々當風流依々老樹
○嚴辰
祥寿紹密拝手

each one of us a unique person, with unique potentialities that often get fouled up by the attempted imposition of standards alien to that nature.

If we can view ourselves—and also tigers and people and plants and even social or business situations—with a nonjudging, open eye, the potentialities of each person, situation, and thing will be freer to develop. And the tiger may lie down with the fat boy. And each of us may live at peace with himself. Millennium.

*

> Watermelons:
> Even they
> Can manage themselves.
> —RANSETSU

Consider the melons of the field. They toil not; they simply sit there enjoying their melonhood.

When Issa returned to his native village for a visit, he found that the flies did not share his perceptions:

> My native place!
> Even flies bite me.

Shiki gives us a glimpse of a vast field at the foot of a range of mountains, with clouds clouding overhead and the tiny figure of a farmer farming:

> As innocently as the clouds
> He tills the field:
> Under the Southern Mountains.

Clouds, mountains, man, fields—fulfilling their own natures, neither dominating nor being dominated. Not apart, yet not together.

To learn the nature of each field we till and then to till it in accordance with its nature—there harmony exists, and creativity.

PLATE 5: Out from somewhere projects a cliff top. Two branches of bamboo appear before our eyes. And a little bird stands quietly, unconcerned with what may be on the mountain or in the bamboo grove behind him or the abyss before him.

What is the significance of the bamboo leaves, or of the bird? Are they beautiful? Are they useful? The eager, categorizing grasshopper-mind struggles to classify them. In vain. Before this moment of eternity frozen in a nonspan of time, this mind falls silent.

The bamboo leaves, the bird, the cliff top *are*. They exist as bamboo leaves, bird, cliff top. This is it. No whence; no whither. In the abysmal void they take their place with the countless forms that rise from that void and sink back into it. Large, small, mobile, immobile—each manifests its own nature.

And so with you. Can you sit as quietly as the bird and the bamboo and the cliff top? Can you feel yourself as a form that has come out of formless energy and is a part of it; that exists in its own right, apart from any of the classifications given to it? Can you be just aware, like the cliff top, the bamboo, the bird, frozen in a nonspan of time? A nonself. A being. A formless form. A . . .

*

On the leafless branch
Perched a crow:
An autumn eve.
                    —BASHO

Another timeless moment for us to savor and incorporate into our very nerve cells.

All creatures!
They squirm about among
The flowers in bloom.
                    —ISSA

Flowers bloom calmly. Human beings squirm restlessly. Well—they bloom; we squirm. That's all, Issa says.

A frog!
Quietly and serenely
He gazes at the mountains.

Issa is actually having a little fun at the expense of a frog and of a presumably somewhat overly "mystical" Chinese poet. And at our expense—if we take our sitting quietly too seriously. Squirming is part of our nature, too.

EVERYTHING

Tenet 3: *Everything exists in relation to other things.*

PLATE 6: At first glance we are likely to see an inhospitable land of rocks and crazily precipitous crags and mountains under a big sky. Cruel. Anti-human. Then we look closer. Some people are walking up a road that winds smoothly between rocks to a village nestled at their right, just beneath a rocky overhang. Yes, a village of houses blending so well with the landscape that they seem a natural part of it. Who could live here? Well, let's see. What's out on the lake? Some people in a boat. So this is probably a village of fishermen living on the lake's bounty. And there's the path again, above and farther to the right, winding up by a series of switchbacks to a tea house nestling in a grove of trees on a point at the top of a cliff, almost at the right edge of the painting.

Instead of a land of inhospitable crags, we find a microcosm filled with an austere but presumably efficient set of interrelationships or ecological transactions. Housing—the trees and rocks. Food—the lake and perhaps soil, well watered by mountain streams and springs. And, to satisfy less material but no less basic human needs, a tea house in a grove of trees, facing a magnificent, ever-changing panorama of mountains and valleys, lake and sky. A place for meditation, for contemplation, for a cup of tea. And, over all, the sky with its life-giving sun and showers.

Now we can let our eyes roam over the picture, taking delight in the heights and depths; in the foreground of rocks and trees and houses and the background of skyshouldering summits; in the shock of the savage cliffs and the peace of the lake waters stretching out illimitably. We can sense the patience of the fishermen in the boat and the anticipation of the people heading either for home or for an hour or two of quiet joy—sitting in the tea house in the pines. Thus have things been for hundreds or thousands of years, in a harmony of relationships that has preserved this mode of life.

*

寺根茅舍竹和梅
賓主相逢心不埃
莫怪門前立談久
渡頭日暮待舡來
　　遠江之雲壑等連六

Detail, Plate 6.

Buson wrote:

> Fallen leaves!
> When the wind blows from the west
> They gather in the east.

It has always been that way and always will be, given the nature of dry leaves and a steady wind.

Even to get a morning drink, Chiyo could not bear to disturb the harmony of the well rope and the morning-glory vine that entwined it during the night:

> A morning glory
> Twined round the bucket:
> I will ask my neighbor for water.

Onitsura wrote:

> A cool breeze;
> A whispering in the pines
> Fills the air.

Sssh! Don't disturb this harmony that Onitsura sensed in a tea house on a cliff top.

PLATE 7: *Everything* is a word with mind-expanding connotations. No one can visualize everything, but this landscape, with its indefinitely vast horizon, suggests the illimitable. Beyond the lake that winds out of sight behind the cliffs lie ranges of mountains and other valleys. And beyond them—is it a mirage?—spreads a long lake at the foot of a range that disappears out of the reach of our mental vision.

On the nearer part of this section of our terrestrial ball we see evidences of geologic action over such a stretch of time that it also disappears out of our imagining. Eons ago our planet's crust wrinkled and shifted mightily. Mountains thrust upward; chasms gaped. Then the rains came and the frosts and the winds. And bacteria and trees with their probing roots. Earthquakes, fires, and floods. And finally, after uncountable billions of events, men. Men walking on the now-quiet soil, gazing at the "changeless" mountains, fishing on the quiet water, living in their wooden houses and pavilions beside body- and spirit-nourishing streams. What an admirable harmony of human and nonhuman nature!

What is the basis for this harmony? Billions of transactions between frost and rock, water and sand, tree and soil, mountains and clouds. Each transaction has been working out according to its Tao—the way things go. The total sum lies before us: this present moment—the result of everything that has gone before. Everything has a cause, and the cause of anything is everything.

How can we fret and stew *sub specie aeternitatis*—under the calm gaze of ancient Tao? The salt of the sea is in our blood; the calcium of the rocks is in our bones; the genes of ten thousand generations of stalwart progenitors are in our cells. The sun shines and we smile. The winds rage and we bend before them. The blossoms open and we rejoice. Earth is our long home.

*

Detail, Plate 7.

Basho's heart went out to the tiny violets growing high up in the mountain pass:

> Violets
> By the mountain path:
> There's something humble about them.

And nature, in another mood, joins him with flying leaves and fleeing animals in a common rout:

> Everything is blown away,
> Even wild boars and I:
> Autumn tempest.
> —BASHO

One day, the story goes, while meditating in his garden with friends, Basho heard a frog jumping into his little pond. Spontaneously he uttered the words which are the second and third lines of the most famous haiku of all. Haiku enthusiasts get from this poem profound intuitions of the mystery at the heart of all things.

> The old pond;
> A frog jumps in:
> Sound of water.

THE SELF

Tenet 4: *The self and the rest of the universe are not separate entities but one functioning whole.*

PLATE 8: Three people are being ferried across the lake. Three wait on the strip of land jutting into the water at the other side, perhaps on their way to the little inn on the opposite shore. In the distance, mountains looming over him, a figure, probably that of a solitary fisherman, sits patiently in his boat. Somewhere in the misty distance streams that feed the lake pour down the mountainsides. Here is an ordered harmony, an indivisible ecology, in which each part needs the others. In this world each self exists as part of the whole and the whole has significance for each self.

We cannot logically say self and nonself are one, since quite obviously the lake and the fisherman are not the same. Just as obviously, however, the lake and the fisherman lose their significance as fish-container and fish-catcher, respectively, without the other. They are not two unrelated entities, but parts of one functioning whole.

In the rhythms of this nine-hundred-year-old picture, we feel the flows of energy passing from self to nonself to self to nonself. Mountains and mists and water and shore, and the inn, the ferry, the people—each person, place, thing is a meeting point at which flows of energy are received and transformed and transmitted. Each is a knot in the cosmic net.

*

Basho expresses this unity in haiku after haiku. At the Great Shrine of Ise, he felt both a spiritual and a sensory influx:

> The fragrance!
> Though I know not
> Whence it comes.

And again, in the next two poems by Basho, the flows of energy, the intercommunications, are quite real though invisible:

> To the path of the sun
> Hollyhocks turn
> In the rains of May.

> Veiled by gray showers,
> Mount Fuji unseen:
> More beautiful today.

PLATE 9: Sitting quietly; doing nothing.

The tree also is sitting quietly, doing nothing. And the rocks and the shrubs; the mountains and the water, the air and the clouds. Actually, all these parts of this cosmos are doing the same thing—being. The tree's cells, millions of them, are performing their various functions. The water is even more active, with four hundred thousand bacteria busy in every spoonful. Inside the quiet sage courses his blood, running through miles of tubes to nourish billions of active cells.

From the cellular point of view—and more basic still, from the electronic point of view—all the beings in this picture are one in their functioning. By sitting quietly, the man is closer to his surroundings than if he were walking around. He is more likely to feel his close relationship with the rest of nature by sitting than by doing anything else. The Buddha opened himself to enlightenment as he sat thus. Probably Jesus was transfigured after sitting in the desert for many days. As our sitting sage brings his verbal and physical movements to a halt, he acts more like the nonanimal part of the universe and quite possibly opens himself to deeply buried intuitions that will enrich his life.

As he looks out and down from his seat on the top of a mountain ledge, his senses are taking in light and sound waves, thermal and olfactory stimuli, pressures from the ground and from the air. That

Plate 8.

unresting computer-transformer, his brain, is creating his entire picture of this part of his cosmos. He is creating his mountains, his waters, his trees and rocks and clouds, which are all part of him since they exist inside his brain.

Walking among the trees, he does not disturb a single grass blade: Swimming in the water, he does not make a ripple.

*

Buson manifests the beauty of the plum tree in blossom:

> Spreading a straw mat in the field
> I sat and gazed
> At the plum blossoms.

Who knows what sights and insights may arise while one is sitting quietly? Here is what Issa saw:

> A dragonfly!
> The distant hills
> Reflected in his eyes.

Here is what Buson heard-saw as he meditated in a quiet mountain retreat:

> A mountain temple;
> A monk's hand missed the bell!
> A faint sound.

The universe creates us; we create our universe. Sitting quietly. Buson's picture of quiet, intent old age is quite different from the youthful dynamism of Basho's airy ballet, in the haiku below, yet both have the quality of intense concentration.

> Two butterflies:
> They dance in the air till,
> Double-white, they meet.

THE SELF [45]

COLLABORATING WITH NATURE

Tenet 5: *Man arises from nature and gets along most effectively by collaborating with nature, rather than trying to master it.*

PLATE 10: Here is a man flat out. Not flat out trying feverishly to make his mark by moving mountains but flat out enjoying the mountains just as they made themselves. His mind is as free of thoughts of making progress as the landscape he views, unmoving, is free of river and village and trees.

The mountains show just a few distant summits above the mists. The valley shows just a little nearby low-lying shore. The shore supports just a few small rocks and a few reeds, their fragile stalks bending earthward. The shallow sampan, its rough hull low in the water, floats a few feet offshore, supporting the prone meditator.

This is a world of horizontals. No seaside amusement park structures thrust their scaffolding up out of the sand. No summit hotels or television antennae pimple the peaks. This man and his forebears have been content to stay on the natural plane, content to contemplate rather than conquer.

The whole vast expanse is full of emptiness, open to the transforming power of his imagination. It exists in him as much as he exists in it. Why should he pollute himself with progress? Why thrust up against when he can level with? His motto is not "After me, the deluge," but rather, "After me, many generations of descendants as happy as I."

*

On stones covered with spring pinks
I'd like a few drinks
And then a good snooze.

— BASHO

Plate 10.

Generations of men had drunk and dozed here before Basho came along. Generations will follow. And the pinks will still garland the stone in spring.

> I am tilling the field
> In the shadow of the hill:
> Not a bird sings.
> —BUSON

Buson evidently did not have his tractor along, or his transistor radio, if he could hear the stillness that intensely.

> Above the mist veil
> From time to time
> The lake lifts a sail.
> —GAKOKU

The boat and its crew are so natural a part of the scene that Gakoku says the lake actually lifts the sail. The tiny boat is almost swallowed up in the immensity of the water, yet it is also buoyed up by the water. It could be overturned by the wind, yet it is propelled to its destination by the wind. Waves, boat, mist—all intimately related parts of one whole.

PLATE 11: What could be a more nearly perfect representation of this tenet than this picture? At first glance you may not see the human beings at all, so small are they, so almost indistinguishable from the mineral and plant forms surrounding them, so infinitesimal under the big sky. Yet they move steadily about their business. This world of mountains and cascades and writhing pines growing out of rocks is also their world. The ocean of air that envelops the mountains and lakes envelops and sustains them. They are part of the harmony of heaven and earth. Here they build their homes and temples, and enjoy contemplating the scenes they find around them.

They do not level mountains nor inundate hundreds of square miles of river valley. They do not conquer, ravage, pollute their land.

In many typical Western paintings, *Homo sapiens* is pictured taking up the larger part of the canvas, with the mountains and lakes and sky serving merely as an inconsequential backdrop to his self-importance. In Zen landscapes, the man-environment proportion shows a sound ecological relationship, in which no element dominates or damages any other. Consequently you are likely to experience a feeling of harmony as you look at this picture (and at others painted with this same insight). The mountain path that tires also supports. The waters that could overwhelm also relieve thirst and facilitate travel. The land-hugging, thatch-roofed houses nestle in the shelter of ravines, perch on humpy vantage points, and become parts of groves, as unobtrusive as their makers. In such a timeless landscape you relax your tensions; you get in touch again with existential basics. You, too, are part of this harmony. Flow with it.

*

Onitsura expresses the nonduality of the two worlds:

> I follow thee:
> A noiseless flower
> In my inmost ears.

He has opened himself to the message from without; the communication takes place effortlessly, spontaneously, and silently.

You can tell from the next haiku that Basho had been looking at Zen landscapes and getting the feel of belonging to the whole:

> My horse clip-clopping
> Over a field . . . Oh-ho!
> I'm part of the picture!

What does the picture in this haiku by Ransetsu express to you?

> Above the pilgrims
> Chanting on a misty road
> Wild geese are flying.

NO EGO

Tenet 6: *There is no ego in the sense of an endlessly enduring, unchanging private soul or personality that temporarily inhabits the body.*

PLATE 12: What a triumph of suggestion is this picture by Sesson of a storm at sea. A few strokes of this Zen priest's brushes have created the evocation of a fierce onshore gale that bends the bare branches of the tree, sends surf crashing on the shore, and drives the frail little boat scudding down the waters, almost burying its nose in the waves. Two men, bowed under the blast, play their necessary parts during the tempest, steering the boat and keeping its rigging secure. The tree has endured many such trials, which after all are only temporary. The edge of the shore sometimes beats back the pounding surf and at other times stretches out warm sands as a playground for children. The little boat and its crew have their moods, too, which are part of the moods of the sea and the wind.

What is the "real" mood of the sea: Is it savagely seeking victims or benevolently providing food for us? What is the "real" nature of the tree: Is it stubbornly strong or gracefully pliant? The boat: Is it a utilitarian vessel to hold a catch of fish or an agile, almost living creation, protecting its crew from the rage of the mighty elements? The men: Are they masters or slaves, casually confident or stoically enduring?

None of these, yet all. What are they really, in themselves? A nonsensical question. What are you? The you that is always the same is fictional. *Fictional* means "created." The fictional you, who has a social security number, a driver's license number, a credit-card number from each of a dozen companies, and so on, does exist unchanged. This person's name is on checks and application forms and letters. This person exists in filing cabinets and computers. But the living you who signs the income-tax form and the living you who signs a love letter are quite different. The person who signs an

Plate 12.

application for a social security number at sixteen is immeasurably different from the one who signs for social security payments at sixty-five. The goof at golf is the panther at Ping-Pong.

As you sit here quietly, enjoy your quiet self. Forget your activist self. Such forgetting is not a denial of real self. There is no real self to deny—a self that persists always in one pattern, one mood, one degree of intelligence, one turn of affection. The living you is always changing. Live now; accept yourself as you are now. There is no one to be always blamed, no one to be always praised. Each moment you are lifted by a different wave, blown by a wind from a different quarter, charmed or threatened by a different coastline. Each moment you are responding differently, as your chemical combinations change and result in different reactions to changing external stimuli. If the winds seem too strong, know that they will subside. If the waves seem too high, remember the calm of the depths below the waves. The tree and shore accept both storm and calm. You also must accept, perforce. Go with what's happening and be part of it, with no ego to set itself apart. You will find accepting much pleasanter than trying to insist that the universe accommodate itself to a certain ego that feels itself to be the eternal, unchanging center of the whole show. This little boat will survive the storm as it suits its motions to the wave's heave and the wind's most furious blast.

*

Otsuji writes:

> Into the cold night
> I spoke aloud. . . . But the voice was
> No voice I knew.

This could be startling to someone who believes that he is always the same person, and that his ego always speaks with the same voice.

> Furue beach in the rain:
> Gray water and gray sand
> Blend without an edge.
> —BUSON

Ardent lovers know they blend without an edge. Do we all actually blend with parts of our surroundings more than we'd like to think? If parts of our environment are also we, where's that so-important ego?

A monk in the mist:
I can see him
By his tinkling bell.
—MEISETSU

Where are the boundaries of the monk's being? And of yours?

PLATE 13: The painter of this picture of a cascade had evidently been impressed by the power and grace of the river in flood. The high waters swirl around the outthrusts of the canyon walls and leap up over the natural dam where the opposing walls almost meet. The masses of water at the foot of the cascade dash up into bubbles and spray and foam. Then they flow downstream in waves that perpetually roll away and are perpetually renewed.

Here lie the mystery and fascination of such a spectacle. The waters continually vanish downstream, to be absorbed by ocean and atmosphere. But the river remains: the patterns of swirls and eddies and waves stay much the same, hour after hour, day after day. The river is eternally different, yet eternally the same.

To be more precise, the actual water pouring down this cascade is never the same; what remains the same is the way we see it. The patterns that are formed inside us as we observe the action of the water stay the same. Of course these patterns remain stable because the rock structures and the nature of the water at "fluid" temperatures is practically unchanging.

Just so, we are inclined to see an unchanging soul or ego because of the relatively unchanging structures of our physical bodies and because of the unchanging nature of our legal entities. Since this ego is only imagined, we can easily postulate for it a stable and eter-

Plate 13.

nal nature. Our desire for security urges us to believe just this. If our ego is the center of our world, the notion that it is ephemeral may make the whole universe seem unstable and temporary.

The price we pay for this illusion of security is the necessity to defend this precious ego from all assaults of its enemies—from slights and insults, from feeling undervalued personally and professionally. We have also the necessity to feel that society should enable us to exploit the great potentialities of this remarkable ego. The pattern of the flow of my ego—my pride, my status, my financial and occupational security, the appreciation of my virtues by my loved ones—must remain unchanged. The price we pay for the illusion of an unchanging soul or ego is our engagement in an unrelenting lawsuit with our environment.

To jettison the belief in such an ego-entity, or soul, is to get rid of the burden of this lawsuit. The water flows—sometimes serenely in wide, quiet places, sometimes dashed through rapids and buffeted on rocks. This flow pleases the artist, enriches the farmer, fills the ocean, rises as vapor over the surface of the earth to fall as rain and snow, feeding the springs which fill the river which flows on. Is the water really the river, or the pleasure, or the enrichment, or the evaporation-precipitation cycle? Not one of these—because all.

It flows. We live.

*

Buson speaks of a flash of lightning:

> Waterdrops from the bamboos
> Flashed
> In the lightning.

Ephemeral. Eternal. Where are those drops now? Somewhere, undoubtedly. In the ocean? In the clouds? In the river rapids?

Basho hears something else among the bamboos that conveys the flow of time:

> The last nightingale is singing
> In the bamboo-shoot thicket
> A song of old age.

Keats called his nightingale immortal, but it was unchanging and eternal only as a pattern, not as an individual. Basho's bird of spring is lingering for one last song in summer's bamboo thicket.

Shiki sees the actual moment living and changing in an apparently unchanging context:

> In the straw-thatched temple
> Of the Saddharma Pundarika
> Cockscombs are blooming.

The cockscombs bloom, the nightingale sings, the lightning flashes, the river flows. We live and love and make patterns and . . . .

TRUE INSIGHT

Tenet 7: *True insight does not issue from specialized knowledge, from membership in coteries, from doctrines or dogmas. It comes from the preconscious intuitions of one's whole being, from one's own code.*

PLATE 14: Here is a painting that delights the mind out of thought. On the sensory level, the subtle and subtly interrelated curves of the tree trunk and limbs, of the nearby coves and the distant bays, of the boat, and of the lotus plants are a dance of forms. On the suprasensory level, the fading away of pictorial details into a throbbing emptiness opens one's imagination.

Behind the creation of such a painting are many years of practice with brushes and ink, years of study of paintings of the same school, years of observation in such surroundings, years of training with Zen masters. Yet we know that for each such masterpiece, a thousand other paintings, now forgotten, have come from a similar background. Only occasionally is great work created, for only occasionally does insight of such a high degree of purity inform technique. Both training and inspiration are necessary, but only when a person's conscious actions are guided by the preconscious intuitions of his whole being does he do his best work.

The man who is viewing the lotus flowers (from a boat just inside the shoreline) may be a painter or a poet or a carpenter or a statesman. At this moment, however, he is not busy acting as a painter or carpenter or serving on a committee. He is presumably opening himself to the sensory input from his surroundings, sitting quietly, apparently doing nothing. But what is going on inside him may result in a great painting or poem, a great piece of cabinetry, a great political decision. Perhaps the painter of this picture was enabled to create this masterpiece by just such meditations.

*

No oil to read by
And so I'm off to bed. . . . Ah!
My moonlit pillow!
    —BASHO

Basho's best moment of that evening was perhaps not reading other people's words but experiencing a shock of esthetic delight at seeing his white pillow gleam in the moonlight. He was not free to delight in the moon's light until the study light went out.

Oh stupid scarecrow!
Under your very stick foot
Birds are stealing rice!
    —YAYU

Yayu's scarecrow is clad in a man's jacket, but something is missing. And the birds know it. It takes more than a Ph.D. degree to make a good scientist or a true teacher.

Their names I know not,
But every weed has
Its tender flower.
    —SAMPU

Hundreds of years ago, Sampu, the humble fishmonger, expressed it.

PLATE 15: There is something free and clean about climbing to a mountain ledge or summit and looking down on the world below. You have left a world of street signs, traffic regulations, beaten paths, a world in which you must constantly intermesh with other people's bodies, needs, assumptions, a world where you hide behind the masks of many roles. Up here you are a whole being. On a cerebral level, you react to the delights of landscape viewing and rock and

plant viewing, opening yourself to such innocent and oceanic feelings as may be aroused. On a "lower" level you react to the utter quiet, the purity of the air, the force of the wind, the pleasant fatigue of the climb, and the relaxation of the well-earned rest.

A somewhat similar escape into wholeness is possible as you sit quietly in your meditation spot. Here you can exclude the problems that demand to be coped with and the socially conditioned assumptions that ordinarily push you around. You become open to the preconscious intuitions that arise from a source we may call "your original nature."

You can see on Jittoku's face a seemingly derisive laugh. He may be showing his amusement at the masquerades which the people in the cities of the plain take so seriously. As he stands by himself, exposed to the winds of the four heavens, he gets a chance to see into the nature of things as it is given to him in particular to see.

*

Simplicity and sublimity are behind this haiku by Basho:

> June comes!
> Mount Arashi
> Lays clouds on its peak.

Here is no fancy, "poetic" language, no specialized technique, no doctrine. Simply a straightforward description of a one-to-one meeting of man and mountain. Simple. Sublimely simple.

What does this vignette by Basho do for you?

> Mossy stone basin
> Standing beside
> The cherry blossoms.

The haiku scholar R. H. Blyth has suggested that the source of the unconsciously mind-quieting effect of looking at cherry blossoms is not so much the beauty of the flowers, but "what their beauty arises from, mindlessness, thusness, being what one is, without affectation or self-seeking." And we could say as much for the mossy stone basin, so heavy and enduring beside the fragile cherry blossoms.

Basho points us toward the creative potentialities we may release if we cleanse ourselves of cravings to be "in" with some doctrine or group.

> The white chrysanthemum:
> Not a speck of dust
> To be seen.

EMPTINESS

Tenet 8: *In emptiness, forms are born. When one becomes empty of the assumptions, inferences, and judgments he has acquired over the years, he comes close to his original nature and is capable of conceiving original ideas and reacting freshly.*

PLATE 16: The painter of this picture, Niten, was a noted swordsman as well as a great painter; hence we should not be surprised at the utter simplicity and directness of the painting. The main stem of the withered tree must have been made with two sure, sweeping strokes of Niten's brush—as sure and sweeping as were his sword strokes. No wavering or wobbling. Second thoughts, wondering, would mean death in combat, failure in painting—failure in expressing with brush and ink the simple directness required for a calm and poised inner posture.

This simplicity is not kin to simplemindedness or to barrenness of imagination. In the ascetic theme set by the fiercely intent bird and withered dead tree, note the humorous touch. Do you see the caterpillar climbing up the stem? A fearless, furry fellow, feeling his way blindly upward, quite possibly to an unexpected dinner engagement with the shrike. Niten's simplicity is the seedbed of an infinite variety and succession of possibilities. This simplicity is akin to what Buddhists call "emptiness."

Notice the seemingly blank background against which the tree and bird stand. Most of the picture is void, empty, yet we feel that this void is, potentially, teeming with images—trees, woods, mountains, clouds, grasses—go ahead and imagine something, and it's there. But at this moment there exist primarily and simply one withered tree, one bird, one caterpillar. Or rather, there exist a few deft, incisive strokes which enable us to create a three-item picture that brings us up straight, concentrated, intense. One-pointed. Simple. All else is pregnant emptiness.

*

Do you get an effect of simplicity from this haiku by Boncho?

> Snow-swallowed valley:
> The river alone painted
> A black, winding line.

Life seems extinct, swallowed up by the inanimate snow crystals. The river is not a live, flowing, purling stream but a painted simulacrum. How much stiller can you get? Here is the stillness of non-life. Emptiness. A piece of calligraphy—one black curving line on white. Yet we know that deep beneath the white snow and black ice, life is potential. And beneath the quiet stillness of a person's sitting lies the potential of vigorous, creative action. But now is the time of quiet, of rest, of recouping of forces, of one-pointedness rather than diversity of action. Of simplicity in its essence. Of emptiness from which will come many new forms.

> Voices of two bells
> That speak from twilight temples:
> Ah! cool dialogue.
> —BUSON

And, if Buson's dialogue is not simple enough for you, consider his camellia:

> A camellia dropped down
> Into the water
> Of a still, dark well.

PLATE 17: If you didn't have the two pavilions and the man in the lower one as clues, you could imagine this to be a picture of any number of things—growths on the sea bottom or in an aquarium, features of the surface of an imagined planet, molds or funguses. You name it and it's yours.

Most of the picture consists of "nothing," of space, emptiness, the void. (And God said, "Let there be forms," and there were forms.) A Zen picture invites you to a godlike activity, invites you to enter into a transaction with it by presenting you with emptiness out of which to create forms. The artist gives you a clue or two, but, like a good haiku writer, he lets you supply your forms and significances out of your "original nature."

As you look at this picture, try not to say anything to yourself. If you suppress all words, you will inhibit the rush of easy inference and conventional assumption. You will feel forms being born inside you while you gaze at one or another feature of the landscape. You may feel almost as if these forms were about to burst out of your head. You may feel the whole empty sky begin to throb with a fullness of light or energy. Be still and know that you IT are God.

*

The poet Sokan made a long spring day out of a spherical void:

> Emerging from a perfect sphere;
> Yet how long it is:
> A spring day.

Basho praises those who resist the easy inference:

> Those who see the lightning
> And think nothing:
> How precious they are!

Daio made such a complex structure of thoughts-feelings out of his New Year's Day that he couldn't express it in words:

> New Year's Day:
> What I feel goes
> Beyond words.

Emptiness, silence, is not nothingness, but fullness. Your fullness.

THINKING AND ACTING

Tenet 9: *Being a spectator while one is also a participant spoils one's performance.*

PLATE 18: The Zen master says, "When you eat, eat; when you sleep, sleep," How many of us have had indigestion from mealtime arguments; how many of us have lain for hours wide awake, throbbing with ideas, fears, hopes, when we have gone to bed to sleep? How many tennis games have been lost by thinking about winning while returning a serve?

The disease of thinking about our actions while we are acting can be particularly virulent in ink painting. Once the brush touches the paper, no erasing is possible. The paper is too absorbent. Before the painter begins, he must have his conception complete, clearly visualized. Once he begins, he must ply his brush without hesitation, without second thoughts, as the swordsman does his sword.

If we study the brush strokes in this painting of the heron, we can understand this. Look at the bird's head. Four brush strokes made it. The bill, a dark straight line; the eye, just a touch of a well-inked brush tip; the head, two light, diffused strokes with the side of the brush. Would you want a millionth of a drop of ink placed differently? A similar strength and economy are visible in the legs and feet. The texture and marking of the bird's feathers are conveyed with essential truth by hundreds of brush strokes. The distant hills probably took only a few seconds to brush in. Yet the suggestion of height and distance and of a wide, hazy intervening valley is irreproachable. Though based on years of study and practice, the execution of this picture must have been totally spontaneous.

This heron and Ryosen's heron (Plate 23, p. 85) both express in their appearance the attitude of being one with what they are doing. Ryosen's heron is in a marsh, hunting, completely intent on stabbing a frog with his rapier-like bill. Tan'an's is standing on a rock while he surveys the valley, perhaps looking for a likely marsh in which to hunt.

The herons, of course, have no language in which to think about themselves and comment on their actions, only man having this peculiar ability to "think about," which also gives us human beings the power to pollute the purity of an action with thoughts about how we are performing. The ink painter, however, does his contemplating and visualizing beforehand. Then he acts. Spontaneously and unreflectingly. Like the herons.

*

I sneezed:
And lost sight
Of the skylark.
—YAYU

Just as Yayu's sneeze impaired the purity of his action, so a "thought about" may spoil a painting, a putt, a performance of any kind.

The beggar!
Heaven and earth
His summer wear.
—KIKAKU

Having no clothes to wear, the beggar goes about quite unselfconsciously, begging for food. Satisfying his need to survive, he cannot afford to divert his attention to the relatively minor problem of being naked.

The long night:
The sound of the water
Says my thought.
—GOCHIKU

The water does not comment on the night or on itself. Its sounds are part of the night—and so is Gochiku.

PLATE 19: One of the inscriptions on this painting is an appreciation by Emperor Ch'ien-lung of China, dated 1760. More than two hundred years ago the head of one of the largest empires in the world found here something to refresh his spirit. Seven hundred years ago, in the Sung dynasty, people preserved and hence presumably treasured this picture, for reasons we may suppose similar to those of Emperor Ch'ien-lung and to those that can move us today.

One of these reasons is undoubtedly the unselfconscious, straightforward simplicity of this bucolic moment. The walking boy is totally absorbed in the bird he is cupping tenderly in his hands. His feet are finding the accustomed way all by themselves. The buffalo are following in complete obedience, as we can see by the slackness of the ropes through their noses. The second little boy is thoroughly relaxed on the buffalo's back, there being no need to use whip or rope. The little calf seems to be happily following his perambulating milk-bar. Even the willow branches are obeying the law of gravity as they point toward the earth.

Responding to this direct simplicity, this freedom from spectator thoughts, we get the feel of Eden before the Fall. The whole scene breathes a spontaneous, "with-it" spirit. The boy wants to treat the little bird tenderly—and he does. The buffalo want to follow the boy to their common destination—and they do. The other boy is interested in expending the least possible amount of thought, talk, and effort in getting where they're all going—and he is.

To be totally absorbed in what we're doing is to use our powers and faculties at their maximum efficiency. As we divert our thrust by standing aside and viewing ourselves in action, to that degree do we lessen our capability and enjoyment. Wondering if we're doing the right thing or the thing right, at the same time that we're doing our thing, inevitably detracts from the doing. There is a time to think about acting and a time to act. They are not the same.

*

Now, as you sit erect, breathing regularly and slowly, just sit erect, breathing regularly and slowly.

So sat some unknown person, simply aware of one sound and one sight:

Plate 19.

A single cricket
Chirps, chirps, chirps,
And is still:
My candle sinks and dies.
                    —ANONYMOUS

Issa didn't ask why his quiet composure had to be assaulted by one fly. He wrote:

One man
And one fly
In a large room.

Basho gives us an unforgettable picture of complete participation in a transaction, unmarred by a comment from either hungry stomach or poetic fancy:

A child of a poor family
Stopped grinding rice
To look at the moon.

THE UNKNOWN

Tenet 10 : *Security and changelessness are fabricated by the ego-dominated mind and do not exist in nature. To accept insecurity and commit oneself to the unknown creates a relaxing faith in the universe.*

PLATE 20: Can you help smiling in sympathy with Ho-tei? Obviously, he is the man who has everything—everything he wants. Also, pretty obviously, all his worldly goods are in the bundle on his back. Here he is, padding along barefoot in a ragged old robe that doesn't quite cover him, not knowing where his next meal will come from nor where he'll sleep tonight. Having committed himself to the unknown, he has accepted his insecure lot; his broad smile shows that he's prepared for anything. If he were dominated by an ego that demanded of life the unchanging maintenance of security, he would have that tight-lipped, frowning, uptight, ulcerous look we see on so many faces today.

Few in our culture can directly imitate this early specimen of the hippie. But can he not be a symbol for us of an ideal state of mind toward which to stretch, as far as our status symbols and mutual-fund certificates will let us? Maybe there is a middle way, a razor's edge, between trusting God and keeping our powder dry. Even as we try to keep our powder dry, we must realize that degrees of humidity vary and that bad storms do occur. To comfort ourselves we build imaginary pictures of eternally dry powder kegs, but such do not actually exist.

Ho-tei has given up such fancies, and by the expression on his face we can tell that he has decided to accept with grace whatever comes by way of food and lodging. Freedom, he seems to be saying, is not getting what you like but liking what you get. He's got a bindle and a smooth path and he likes the whole situation.

*

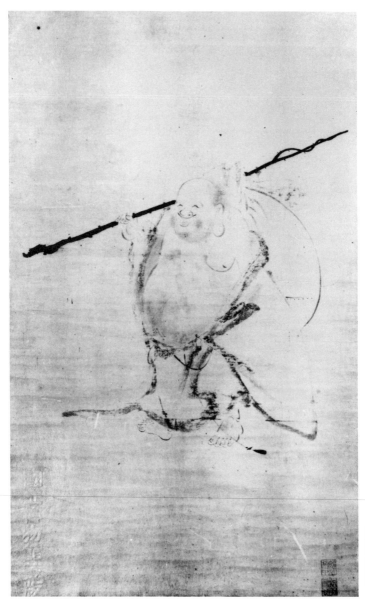

Did Basho's horse anticipate a feast of beauty?

> The rose of Sharon
> Bloomed by the roadside:
> A horse ate the flowers.

Every photographer has experienced Chora's frustration:

> The moon;
> When I look at it—clouds:
> When I don't look—clear.

Can one seek security from being lonely?

> Loneliness!
> It, too, is joy:
> An autumn eve.
>   —BUSON

PLATE 21: Let's imagine that the artist had in mind the very top of one of those vertical peaks so common in mountain landscapes of the Sung dynasty. On the outer edge of a narrow ledge just below the topmost rock stands a heron. Behind him, protected by the overhang, are a few bits of vegetation and perhaps a nest of sticks. The rest is a sea of mists swirling in an infinitely deep abyss. Into this abyss the standing heron peers while the flying heron circles above, perhaps trying to ride the turbulent wind-currents in to a landing on the ledge.

What a habitat! Exposed to the elements at their least merciful; far from shelter and perhaps food; dizzyingly distant from the security of a quiet, fertile valley! Yet there must have been something about this site that made the birds feel they could survive here. The fact that they are indeed surviving here justifies their "faith."

The bird gliding on thin air above the abyss can symbolize the act of committing oneself to the unknown out of one's faith in the universe. The bird has been shaped—through a long evolution of its species—by the gravitational and meteorological conditions of this planet, and now these conditions sustain it. What chance had this species, a million years ago, of surviving to this moment? Very little, yet by evolving in an ever-changing environment, it did survive.

We look into this abyss and shudder at the thought of the awful height that a clearing of the mist would reveal. The abyss is like our future—inchoate, full of potential shocks, alarms, disasters. How shall we react? Fearfully trying to build unbreachable safeguards, so we can live unchanging lives behind our impregnable lines of defense? Or walking on into the mists, trusting that our forces and resources will continue to sustain us, as the air currents carry the skillfully soaring birds.

If we abandon the feeling that we are separate, fragile egos in unreliable bodies and a dangerous, alien universe, we will naturally take on the feeling that we ourselves are the nondual combination, the organism-environment complex. Many dangers undeniably exist, but if the combination were not primarily favorable to survival, we wouldn't be here. The odds are in our favor. To struggle for an unchanging security and to think we have achieved it may well alter the odds against us. We are better off accepting the fact that the world gives no annuity guaranteeing us life, health, and happiness. The Fates, said the Romans, find a path for the willing and betray the unwilling. "Life is what happens to us while we are making other plans."

*

At the end of an arduous eight-month journey Basho wrote (with surprise?):

> Still alive
> At the journey's end:
> A late autumn eve.

Shiba experienced an existential joy in a cheerless situation:

Plate 21.

Happiness:
Waking, alive again,
In this gray world of winter rain.

Shiki and his friend, lost in the fog, just kept on rowing:

Into fog, through the fog
We rowed. Then:
The wide sea—so blue, so bright!

THE MOMENT

Tenet 11: *One can live only in the present moment.*

PLATE 22: A thousand years are only a day in the life of fish. The ancestors of this underwater creature looked the same to their brothers and to their predators, a thousand years ago, as this big carp does now. The millennia pass and the big round eyes stare at the various shapes in this corner of the subaqueous universe. The tails and fins perform the same constant movements; each fish is perpetually poised for the life-preserving flight or attack.

In the liquid currents the grasses sway, responsive in each of a billion moments to the slightest movement in their medium, drinking in the nutriments from sun and water. The curves of their stems repeat the undulant curves of a fish's body.

In this hushed, soundless, submarine corner of the living world, time—the time of commuters, of airlines, of count-downs—seems not to exist. Instead, there exists only the organismal moment—the beat of the heart, the inflow and outflow of oxygen-bearing water, the reflex action of fin muscles, the movements of stem- and leaf-cells. Each action lasts its moment and then is no more. There is no past on which each fish broods, nor any future which makes its heart beat faster. The fish and the grasses live suspended in the watery moment, at one with the environment that sustains them.

When we human beings can stop using language or when we can use it to cope simply and purely and only with the present moment, we find that the quality of our living is changed. In the midst of a fast volley of tennis, or when we stop suddenly by a pond in spring and listen to hundreds of peepers, or as we watch a spaceship take off and gather speed at the start of its lunar journey—at such moments we are at one with ourselves. All our forces are concentrated unreflectingly, unselfconsciously, on the playing, listening, watching. We are living at our best.

When we sit in meditation with this same unselfconscious concentration, we also generate organismal joy. This heightened quality of living affects all our activities.

When we can move through life eating, sleeping, working, making love, without, as we do so, dwelling on the past or in the future, then we can live with all possible vigor or joy. Organismically, we can live only in the present. We should avail ourselves of this wisdom of our organism.

*

Issa noted, in the unselfconscious moment of absorption, a heightened quality of life:

> Cherry trees:
> Contemplating their beauty,
> Strangers are like friends.

Buson gives us another picture of at-one-ness:

> An old fisherman:
> Unalterably intent
> In evening rain.

PLATE 23: Poised for a lightning thrust, this heron's whole being is concentrating on one objective: Get that frog. His long powerful neck is bent like a spring; his body is leaning forward to provide mass for the attack; his eyes are fixed unwinking on his prey; his weapon, that long, pointed bill, is aimed and ready. For him there exists no past or future—only the present. As we look at him, time seems to stop; we, too, lean forward, frozen in an inner attitude of readiness, living completely in the NOW.

How refreshing, to live concentratedly in the instant. To give over regrets, anticipations, worries, reflections, and reflections on reflections. To focus on the job at hand. How refreshing, and how loosening of prejudices and inhibitions. We are enabled to enter into a more productive transaction with what we are trying to do.

Actually, like the heron, we can live only in the moment—on the organismal level. We cannot now live yesterday; we cannot now live tomorrow—or even the next minute. But, unlike the heron, we possess another dimension—that of words—and on that dimension we can project ourselves imaginatively into the past and the future. This ability has its delights and its dangers, both of which can distract us from living effectively in the moment.

Sometimes, of course, it is the job of this moment to plan for a future, using the experience of the past. Thus may we use the moment wisely. But it is this moment we are using. This is how we hunt; we make plans and profit by feedback. But once the hunt is over, we should leave the prey to our digestive tracts.

Living thus one-pointedly, our bodies are full of light. The thrust of living in a whole, alert fashion wields us like the dart of the heron's bill. We move in harmony with our total forces. To each moment, its own.

*

> The spring breeze:
> How white the heron is
> Among the pines.
> —BASHO

Here is a snowy heron in another posture, flying like a white spirit through a grove of dark pine trees. Moment by moment he appears and disappears. If we are not alert to look in a different spot each moment, we shall miss him.

> The dragonfly
> Perches on the stick
> Raised to strike him.
> —KOHYO

Here is super-alertness! Kohyo's dragonfly has sized up the situation in a lightning flash. How can the man strike at him if he is sitting on the fly swatter? If the man moves the swatter, the drag-

Plate 23.

onfly gets the cue to flee. If the man does not move the swatter, well, he's perfectly safe. He has preserved his life by acting spontaneously, in reflexive response to his total input of stimuli. No second thoughts for him.

Lightning flash:
Still water gleams bright
Between the dark trees.
—SHIKI

If Shiki had not been as alert as a hunting heron, he would not have seen this vision. Life's vital moments flash upon us like the swiftly changing projections of a tachistoscope, testing our perceptions. If we walk through the dark wood of life thinking of the past and the future, we shall miss the bright actualities revealed by life's lightning flashes.

WORDS

Tenet 12: *Living process and words about it are not the same and should not be treated as equal in worth.*

PLATE 24: Here is a picture of demoniac energy in action. The monk tearing up the papers has a look of fiendish glee. What is he tearing up? A scroll of Buddhist scriptures. In any religion but Zen such an action would surely be regarded as evil. Yet this is a picture of Hui-neng, the first great Chinese Zen master, painted by a Zen-inspired artist who was one of China's greatest masters of brush and ink.

What's going on? What's the Zen point?

Perhaps a couple of exchanges between Zen masters and their disciples will furnish a pertinent background. Here is one, as it was told by the Zen scholar D. T. Suzuki:

> A monk asked Hui-neng, the sixth patriarch of the Zen sect in China, "Who has attained to the secrets of Wobai?"
> Hui-neng: "One who understands Buddhism has attained to the secrets of Wobai."
> Monk: "Have you then attained them?"
> Hui-neng: "No, I have not."
> Monk: "How is it that you have not?"
> Hui-neng: "I do not understand Buddhism."*

Another exchange reported by Suzuki tells how, in attempting to get an answer to his wondering about the essence of Buddhism, a monk once asked:

> "What is the meaning of the First Patriarch's coming from the West?"
> Master Shih-t'ou answered, "Ask the post that's standing over there."
> The monk replied, "I don't understand what you mean."

* *Essays in Zen Buddhism,* first series (London: 1970), pp. 264–65.

Thereupon Master Shih-t'ou ended the colloquy by saying, "My ignorance far exceeds yours."*

Here we have two Zen masters, living embodiments of Buddhist insight and enlightenment, disclaiming any understanding of Buddhism and even of their own replies to inquiries about it.

Understandings and discussions must be phrased in words. But the words of any language fall far short of mirroring the vital processes of life. Words of wisdom have no meaning until one's own experience gives them meaning. Each person must be enlightened by his own experience. The Zen masters try to give their disciples experiences that will shock them into this realization.

Tearing up the holy books of one's religion is shocking to a respectful student of that religion. But from the Zen point of view this is an ideal situation to paint, impressing on the sensitive viewer the difference between the inner meanings of a way of life and verbal descriptions of it.

Not only may the idea behind the painting contribute to insight, but so may the technique of the painter. The brushwork itself projects the contrast between the intense energy of living process and the dead papers fluttering in the wind. The strokes are mostly short and straight or angular. Some are very black and some very light, with a startling, staccato effect like that of a series of shouts. The angular figure has one leg raised, showing the intensity of the emotion behind the tearing of the sutra scroll. The monk seems to be almost dancing—with rage at the pretensions of writers, and with glee that he has the power to tear the writings to pieces.

*

As Soseki discovered, even butterflies confuse words and things:

> Butterfly! These words
> From my brush are not flowers,
> Only their shadows.

* Adapted from *Essays in Zen Buddhism*, second series (London: 1970), p. 231.

Issa found a nonverbal and nonhuman communicator who spoke to his feelings:

> Plumes of pampas grass
> Tremble in every wind:
> A lonely heart.

Basho tells what happens to symbols of insight and wisdom:

> The carved god is gone:
> Dead leaves alone foregather
> On the temple porch.

PLATE 25: Here we see a poor befuddled monkey reaching for what he thinks is the moon. He sees a reflection of the moon in the pool and tries to grasp it. If he ever stretches enough to reach the water with his right paw, what will happen? He'll get a wet paw and he'll destroy the reflection, which will be a puzzlement to his benighted, wordless brain. If he could speak, you can be sure he'd blame his failure on something outside himself—ill luck or fate. Not on himself.

Of course the fault does lie in him, because he mistakes the reflection of the moon for the moon itself, just as human beings mistake the symbol for the reality. This failing in Zen students is one that their teachers hit at hard and often. Hundreds of stories tell of the ways Zen teachers impress on their students the primacy of the deed, the primacy of living process. Some stories tell of students being struck, reproved, made fun of, sent off to do some manual work to stop their verbalizings about religion and enlightenment. Other stories tell of nonsense-answers to such inquiries.

D. T. Suzuki recorded such an instance in connection with Joshu, a Zen master. A monk asked him, "I read in the sutra that all things return to the One, but where does this One return to?" The master

replied, "When I was in Tsing province a robe I had made weighed seven *chin*."*

We can imagine that monk going off to try a wordless meditation for a while after that rebuff.

The trouble is that language does play an important part in structuring our ideas about living, and hence our ways of behaving. Since we get our language from our elders and peers, who are full of misconceptions, we are likely to see life less than truly when we come to shape our own reactions. Words put a screen between reality and us. Our inner wisdom formulates the patterns of the language we learn to use before we ever have a teacher. It shapes and maintains our brain and all the rest of us. Surely it has a better chance to guide our conscious doings if we learn to turn off the flow of words and open ourselves frequently to its guidance.

Whatever we say about anything is merely what we say about it; it is not the same as the thing itself. If we hope to tap our potentialities for true insights and true action, we have to act on a quite different premise from the one in this monkey's head. And if we cannot, at will, stop the flow of words, the flow of inferences and judgments and poorly founded speculations, then we should at least become aware that life is other than and sometimes quite different from what we say about it.

*

Silence. A cool evening.
Thinking pleasant thoughts
With a friend.
—HYAKUCHI

Hyakuchi and his friend had evidently learned a lesson in productive communication.

A raging sea!
Above Sado Island lies
The Milky Way.
—BASHO

* Adapted from *Essays in Zen Buddhism*, second series (London: 1970), p. 94.

Basho gives us a feel of the difference between two worlds; the world of discussions and debates, and the world of living processes that make possible the existence of the thunderers of words. The noisy theological debates of the Middle Ages are dead but the silent genes of many of the debaters are alive and shaping people's destinies today.

> A hundred gourds
> Born
> From the mind of one vine.
> —CHIYO

And, Chiyo might have added, without using one word.

THEORIES

Tenet 13: *When we perceive the incongruity between theories about life and what we feel intuitively to be true on the nonverbal, nonjudging plane, there is nothing to do but laugh.*

PLATE 26: Eight hundred years ago Toba, a Japanese artist (who was also a Buddhist priest), painted a long scroll with many scenes of apes and frogs and rabbits and deer frolicking. Some of the frolicking was pure animal spirits; some of it was tongue-in-cheek mimicking of human behavior. In this scene, for example, a frog sits cross-legged in a "sacred" place, as if he were the Buddha or a Buddhist abbot. He is sitting on a lily pad, with a reredos of large leaves—a parody of the Buddha's lotus throne and sacred cobras. An ape is kneeling before His Pseudo-Holiness dressed in a priest's robe—which doesn't actually fit him any too well. The frog stares with supersolemnity, making the Buddha's teaching gesture with his right "hand." The ape piously extends a floral offering, together with some presumably religiose sentiments.

What are we to make of this seeming sacrilege? Was Priest Toba an idol breaker? Or was he taking an artful way of telling us not to worship our religious symbols? One Zen master is reported as saying, "If you meet the Buddha on the street, kill him." This hyperbole carries a meaning like Toba's in the picture of the ape-priest bowing before the frog-Buddha. Don't treat your religious symbols as if they were the realities they symbolize. Don't mistake the reflection of the moon for the moon. If you feel inclined to worship an external being or symbol, even the Buddha, have a good laugh at yourself.

Only a human being can create symbols. Only a human being can laugh at himself for mistaking the role of his symbols. Is there a better way than laughter to remind us that the Sabbath, with all its laws and symbols and shibboleths, was made for man and not vice

Plate 26.

versa? Are you letting your socially conditioned ways of seeing life make a monkey of you?

Master Lin-chi's reply to a monk seeking to hear in words the essence of Buddhism reveals the typical Zen attitude toward such an attempt to catch the fish of meaning in a net of words. The monk had asked, "What is the meaning of Bodhidharma's coming from the West?" The master's reply, in D. T. Suzuki's version of the story, was, "If there were any meaning, no one could save even himself."*

Toba says the same thing through his loquacious ape and solemn frog. Those who don't know, tell; those who know—intuitively and profoundly—don't tell. They just laugh at any attempt to express the meaning of life in words.

*

Sokan seems to have had the same feeling about frogs—and self-important people—that Toba had:

> Fawning fat frog you,
> Spreading damp hands on inlaid floor.
> Croaking courtier.

Issa half-affectionately attends to a creature most people are conditioned to despise:

> Surprise!
> A snail at my feet.
> When did he get here?

Sampu hugs his quilt to him under a beautiful moon.

> Moon so bright for love!
> Come closer, quilt,
> Enfold my passionate cold!

Sampu's statement tells us nothing—at least nothing very sen-

* *Essays in Zen Buddhism*, second series (London: 1970), p. 193.

sible—in so many words. But as we let his images percolate deep inside us, we get a notion of how he feels on this cold, clear night, lying feverish, perhaps, on his bed. The painful incongruity between what he imagines experiencing in such a place on such a night and what he is actually experiencing evokes this burst of black laughter.

Plate 27: Shohaku's almost life-size painting of three friends walking across a bridge is based on an old story. Once upon a time there was an abbot who vowed he would never again walk across the bridge that spanned the chasm between his monastery and the outside world. One day two friends came to visit him. They all had a big feast together. When the time came to say goodbye, the three of them were talking so fast and so merrily that, before they knew it, they had all crossed the bridge. When the two visitors said to the abbot, "Hey, you just broke your vow," he laughed even more merrily. The three friends then had to grab each other to keep from falling into the gorge, they laughed so hard.

It is this moment that Shohaku has captured with his brush—the moment of crisis, in which the abbot would either be struck with guilt and dismay at having broken his vow or be tremendously amused at the way life triumphs over man's plans and verbalizings.

One of the most fundamental concepts in Zen is symbolized by "*Mu.*" This sound or word is a general negative sign and is often used in contexts which signify that our ideas of how life should go are not necessarily the way life does go. If events occur that are at variance with our blueprints, Zen tells us to swing with the punches, accept—with a curse or a laugh—and go on with the dance.

Many of us tend to think of life as a parade, something planned exactly in advance to produce a preordained effect on both participants and spectators. A parade is meant to be a triumph of artifice over nature. The Zen person, feeling himself to be part of nature, thinks of life rather as a dance, a dance in which one moves joyfully and spontaneously. Its value lies in the dancer's joy, not in the crea-

Plate 27.

tion of a particular reaction in the spectators nor in the satisfaction gained from following slavishly a pattern someone has created beforehand.

Isn't this the spirit of this painting? Instead of three dignitaries bowing ceremoniously to each other, concealing behind impassive facades their dismay at the breaking of a vow, we see three hilarious old rascals warmly attached to each other, physically and psychologically. They are just tremendously amused by the incongruity between what man proposed and what life disposed.

*

Basho, finding his larder empty as an unexpected visitor drops in, reacts with a laugh:

> The small size of
> The mosquitoes:
> My best hospitality.

Issa is equally philosophical:

> If the times were good:
> "One more of you sit down,
> Flies around my food."

Kyorai submitted with grace to the natural law governing the movements of his head in the bitter cold:

> The cold!
> I just can't look up
> At the crescent moon.

One cannot always enjoy what one plans to enjoy. So? . . . Laugh. Swear. Write a haiku. And walk on.

ZEN ART

Tenet 14: *Zen art has this characteristic quality, that it can fuse delight in a work of visual art, knowledge of life, and personal experiences and intuitions into one creative event.*

PLATE 28: The dragon glaring at us out of the depths of this cosmic streaming is one of nine painted on one long scroll by Ch'en Jung over seven centuries ago in China. The whole scroll is filled with such scenes of wild energy. Gigantic waves and spinning maelstroms dash off long fingers of spume. Just such a coiling and such a writhing exist in spiral nebulae, in atoms, and in human hearts and minds. Out of such wild energy came life, including human life. And in wildness, as Thoreau said, is the preservation of life.

In the primeval storm of the elements lives this dragon, a coiling, writhing being who symbolizes the energy that created and preserves life. He is an immortal being, as energy is immortal, an archetypal image of that within each of us which makes our existence more than ingestion and excretion. His claws and horns and savage sideways look do not charm or reassure us. They are fearsome, like the billows of mist and water in which he makes his home.

What transaction may we make with such a picture?

First, if we study the brushwork, we will be awed by the mastery it reveals—the sureness of stroke in the whorls and waves, the combination of meticulous attention to detail and spontaneity in the foamy edges of the mist fingers, the exactness of representation of the dragon's face and body, so scrupulous yet so natural, as they blend unobtrusively with the rest. No wonder Ch'en Jung's Nine Dragons Scroll has been treasured for over seven hundred years by Taoist chief priests and by Chinese emperors.

Second, we can treasure it, as the Taoists did, for its symbolic effect. It expresses their feeling and understanding of the ineffable power and mystery of life. And it gives a shape to the tempests that we sometimes feel in ourselves, tempests that toss our reason and will like chips on ocean waves.

Zen art has this characteristic quality, that it can fuse delight in a work of visual art, knowledge of life, and personal experiences and intuitions into one creative event. Such an event can bring inner structures into being that will help each person's own unconscious achieve the insight that will be liberating for that particular person. Such a transaction is not achieved easily. Ch'en Jung contributed his profound insight and his plastic power. To do our part, we must open our depths to contemplation of this ancient Taoist symbol.

*

Gyodai conveys some of the wildness of this planet in a motion-less vignette:

> In the cold sky of dawn
> Only a single pine tree
> On the peak.

Basho's image is dynamic:

> The sea darkening:
> Oh, voices of the wild birds
> Crying, whirling, white.

Basho uses both the animal and the insensate worlds to give us another image, helping us feel the awe and mystery of cosmic wildness:

> Lightning flashing:
> Beyond the darkness darts
> A night heron's scream.

Plate 28.

PLATE 29: Here, in a few brushstrokes by Liang K'ai, is an immortal portait of the immortal "Prince of Chinese Poets." Li Po seems to be looking far into the distance. Psychic distance? Physical? Both? Perhaps he was watching his friend, Meng Hao-jan, on his way to Yang-Chou, as he wrote twelve hundred years ago:

> You have left me behind, old friend, at the Yellow Crane Terrace
> On your way to visit Yang-Chou in the misty month of flowers;
> Your sail, a single shadow, becomes one with the blue sky,
> Till now I see only the river, on its way to heaven.*

What is there about this painting that hypnotizes us? We project upon an almost shapeless robe a noble dignity of stance, solid without being still or rigid, proud without being pompous. The fine straight brush strokes that limn his face and eyes imply clarity and keenness of vision. The almost fierce gaze communicates a feeling that he is his own man, that he calmly knows his own worth. Here is a man who will stand and watch his departing friend's sail until it becomes one with the blue sky on the river that flows to heaven. Here is a man who, like Keats, feels poignantly the transience of "Joy, whose hand is ever at his lips, bidding adieu," but who accepts the fact without regretting it. Here is a man—well, we can go on and on, seeing in these few black ink strokes progressive revelations of what proud things it can mean to be human. And as these intuitions arise during our contemplation, we gradually grow into this great work of Zen art. A spiritually significant event occurs. Our own experiences and dreams, the genius of Liang K'ai, the personality of Li Po—all of these fuse. We are more than we were.

*

Basho offers us a synesthetic stimulus at once strong and delicate:

> As bell tones fade,
> Blossom scents take up the ringing:
> Evening shade!

* "A Farewell to Meng Hao-jan on His Way to Yang-Chou," from *The Jade Mountain: A Chinese Anthology* (New York: 1929), trans. Witter Bynner.

Delicate and soft is Kikaku's picture:

> A full moon:
> On the tatami
> Falls the shadow of pines.

Some unknown haiku writer gives us an unforgettable vignette of patient womanhood, a quick glimpse that can go on and on reverberating for a long time:

> As she washes rice
> Her smiling face is briefly
> Lit by a firefly.
> —ANONYMOUS

The sweet young woman, the noble poet, the pine-tree calligraphies, the resonant, fragrant air—all transformed by art and by our imaginations into spiritually significant events.

TRANSACTIONS WITH THE WORLD

Tenet 15: *Each of us develops into a unique individual who enters into unique transactions with the world as it exists for him.*

PLATE 30: Bodhidharma is traditionally regarded as the founder of the Zen sect of Buddhism. How many founders of religions or religious sects are pictured by their followers looking like this? One expects either an otherworldly serenity (Gautama Buddha) or an otherworldly patience under persecution and suffering (Jesus Christ).

Here we have a thoroughly human, rather crusty, curmudgeonly old fellow. A severe hippie type, looking askance at us as if we'd just said something that simply convinced him that it would be a long time before we'd be firmly on the right track. Bald, bearded, an earring in a pierced ear, he looks more like a pirate than a saint.

Perhaps he does have something of the pirate in him, in the sense that he has carried freedom of enterprise to its limit. He put a millennium-old religion on an unexplored track, leaving behind the old maps of Buddhist territory. He set out on an inner voyage, seized his prize, and then realized that by its very nature he couldn't give it to anyone else. His was a unique kind of prize; each follower must find his own. For Bodhidharma believed that each person develops into a unique individual whose transactions with the world of his own perceptions and explorations exist uniquely for that individual. The kingdom of heaven is within, and since each within differs from every other, each heaven is different. No one can be saved by anyone else; no one's revelation is valid for anyone else.

The story of Bodhidharma's meeting with Emperor Wu of Liang exemplifies the personality we may deduce from this portrait. The Chinese emperor described to his missionary visitor all the Buddhist monasteries and temples he had built and endowed and then asked what merit he had accumulated to his karmic account.

"No merit at all!" replied Bodhidharma abruptly and impoliticly.

Emperor Wu, taken aback, asked, "Then what is the sacred doctrine's first principle?"

"It's just empty; there is nothing sacred," was Bodhidharma's reply.

Logically and a little bitterly Emperor Wu asked, "In that case, who are you to stand before us?"

Bodhidharma, pulling the rest of the rug out, replied, "I don't know."*

*

Dansui describes an independent person:

> Even for the Emperor
> He will not lift his hat:
> Unmoving scarecrow.

Bodhidharma moved or not, according to the dictates of his own nature:

> The heavy leaf
> Falls of its own will
> On this silent windless day.
> —BONCHO

Boncho's autumn leaf moves in response to the condition of its own cells, not waiting to be blown by the next wind that comes along.

Basho's skylark is similarly inner-directed:

> The skylark
> Sings in the field:
> Free of all things.

* Adapted from *The Way of Zen*, by Alan Watts (New York: 1959), p. 91–92, and from *Essays in Zen Buddhism*, second series, by D. T. Suzuki (London: 1970), p. 189.

Plate 31.

PLATE 31: What a variety of scenes and people is evident in this landscape. In the right foreground is a hamlet of humble homes, probably of fishermen. A tea house and pavilion extend over the water near the end of the peninsula. In the upper right we glimpse a group of large buildings on the shoulder of a hill—a monastery or a wealthy man's compound. In the mountain defile at the left is a building that may be an inn where the travelers going up the path will stay the night, listening, as they fall asleep, to the rush of the cataract emptying into the lake below. A ferry and three fishing boats are on the lake.

We can assume from what we see that there are fishermen, a ferry-boatman, travelers, enjoyers of tea and vistas, innkeepers, maids, wives and children, monks, maybe a sage or poet. Each one of these people is experiencing a different picture of this world of water, crags, trees, beaches, meadows, cascades. The fisherman is assessing the temperature, roughness, and depth of the water as he concentrates on making a catch. The travelers are watching the path for rocks and holes and stopping frequently to catch their breath as well as to enjoy looking at the pools and falls. The two friends drinking tea together in the pavilion may be enjoying the landscape as we are, watching with a godlike detachment the complex interrelationships of human and nonhuman elements in the scene.

Who has the best view, the best understanding, the best transaction with this segment of our planet? The answer, of course, is "no one." Or "everyone." Each person is differently constituted from every other; each person's experiences, needs, expectations, motivations are somewhat different; where each person stands or sits is different. And hence each person's world is different.

If we assume these radical differences, then we must assume that each person's understanding of life, each person's path to serenity, to being at one with what is inside him and what is outside him, is different. Ultimately, then, each of us must have faith in his own capacity to deal with life on the psychic plane, just as we have in matters of breathing air, digesting food, healing wounds, and interpreting language sounds.

As a certain jazz musician once said about the meaning of a piece of music, "If you gotta ask, you'll never get to know."

*

In the silent dusk
Nightingales begin their song:
Good! The dinner gong!
—BUSON

Buson's needs and expectations at that moment made the dinner gong sound sweeter to him than the nightingales' trill.

But Yaha wasn't hungry:

The temple grounds:
The nightingale begins his trill:
Fui! Peanut vendor!

Issa had a remarkable ability to imagine the fantastically different transactions that an individual of another order of life might be having with the "same" event Issa himself was experiencing:

Bedfellow cricket,
Beware of local earthquakes:
I must turn over.

The cricket has his own—unique—transactions, too.